Land of Laura

DE SMET, SOUTH DAKOTA
Insider Travel Guide to
Laura Ingalls Wilder's Little Towns

SANDRA HUME

NOT THE CRITIC PRESS LLC

www.littlehousetravel.com

Cover Design by Julie Jones

Published by Not the Critic Press LLC
www.notthecriticpress.com
First Printing, 2016
Revised, 2017
Revised, 2025

Library of Congress Control Number: 2016907668
ISBN 978-1-945070-09-9 (Print)
ASIN B01EXKAORQ

All information in this guide is believed to be true. Any factual errors are purely the fault of the author.

To Laura. And Rose. Of course.

TABLE OF CONTENTS

FOREWORD

LITTLE HOUSE® FANS GROW UP. They have children. They share their affection for their favorite books. And if they're lucky, their children adopt this affection. Even better, the cycle may even repeat with the generation to follow. That's why above all, *Land of Laura* is a travel series for families. Single adults or even couples could glean enough valuable information from this guide to make reading it worthwhile, but the majority of my experience in traveling to Laura's homesites is with kids.

But let's start at the beginning: What's a "homesite"? Laura Ingalls Wilder originally wrote eight books that together make up the Little House® series. The series is autobiographical, following the life she and her family actually led as they moved from place to place in the late-1800s pioneering Midwest. Each place she wrote about—Pepin, Wisconsin; Independence, Kansas; Walnut Grove, Minnesota; and De Smet, South Dakota—actually existed, and her legacy there is preserved and honored. Such places are known to fans as "homesites." Malone, New York, which she wrote about in *Farmer Boy*, was the childhood home of her husband, Almanzo, and is also considered a homesite. (Smaller homesites exist at places she lived briefly in her adulthood such as Westville, Florida and Spring Valley, Minnesota.)

There is also one childhood homesite she did not write about in the series: Burr Oak, Iowa, where her family lived between two separate stints in Walnut Grove. And Mansfield, Laura's home of over sixty years, is where she wrote her book series (and the museum there, along with the preserved farmhouse she and Almanzo created, is newly updated and fantastic).

i

As all parents eventually learn, a vacation's level of success is often dependent on one common denominator: the satisfaction of the kids. If the kids ain't happy, ain't nobody happy. So *Land of Laura* is for people like me: parents who love Laura's books and who want to make the most of traveling to her homesites with kids (who may or may not love the books). I've thrown in a few tips for reluctant males as well, should you have to bring one along.

When traveling I embrace a know-before-you-go mentality. My plans have plans. Because people read travel guides in sections, if something is important, I'll repeat it. Restaurants and other businesses come and go, so although I may offer opinions on restaurants or lodging I've experienced personally, always check before you arrive for reviews or updates on closures.

Because information changes often, particularly with restaurants that operate on razor-thin margins in uncertain times, I've refrained from including hours of operation for any business outside of a general idea. Most busiensses have websites or Facebook or Instagram pages that keep you updated. It's wise to do everything you can to verify before you go.

In fact, here's a tip: In small towns like those Laura lived in, the local newspaper is still a primary driver of communication. Notices in the newspaper can often be more accurate and timely than anything else. (It's where you might find out, for example, that your chosen eatery for the evening is closed for a wedding.) Subscribe to the electronic edition of the *Kingsbury Journal* ($50 for the online version at last check, but it could have gone up) in advance of your trip to South Dakota, for example, or pick one up while you're in town to discover what might be going on—or not going on—during your stay.

Bear in mind that you won't find many if any references to the TV show from the 1970s. The show has its own audience and is compelling in its own right. But Laura's actual hometowns bear little resemblance to what was portrayed on TV. Further, it's valuable to note that Laura herself changed some names or simply remembered facts wrong so not everything mentioned in the books did in fact exist the way she said it did.

Throughout the Land of Laura guides I reference dozens of businesses, attractions, and points of interest in and around the location of the homesite I am writing about. All of these are listed at the end of the guide in **APPENDIX: RESOURCES**.

Now let's roll the old chariot along.

INTRODUCTION
DE SMET, South Dakota

WINTER WAS COMING. As the crisp air descended over the tallgrass prairie, a wagon inched the last half-mile towards the newly-established town of De Smet, Dakota Territory. It was the final piece of a journey begun earlier that year when the Ingalls family left Walnut Grove, Minnesota, for points west. It was 1879. Laura Ingalls, twelve years old, ran ahead of the wagon that carried her sisters and parents, beating her entire family to the Surveyors' House, their first winter lodging in the town she would call home for—more or less—the next fifteen years.

For decades Laura Ingalls Wilder fans the world over have approached De Smet with the same excitement building in their own chests. They were going where Laura lived.

De Smet, the setting for the last half of Laura Ingalls Wilder's series—*By the Shores of Silver Lake*, *The Long Winter*, *Little Town on the Prairie*, and *These Happy Golden Years*, plus the series' posthumous addition, *The First Four Years*—is like Mecca for her fans. Five books take place in this small South Dakota town. It's where Laura taught calves to drink from a bucket. Where she studied alongside her best friends Mary Power and Ida Brown. Where the dashing Almanzo Wilder first noticed her and walked her home. Where her skirts were let down and her hair put up as girlhood fell away and schoolteaching began. Where she waited on Sunday afternoons, watching the corner of Pearson's Livery Barn from her claim shanty south of town for Almanzo to arrive for their weekly buggy rides.

What do *you* remember the most about De Smet? The Loftus Store? The Big Slough? The grassy hills of Laura and

Mary's walks? Singing school? Church with Reverend Brown? Tay Pay Pryor's errant foot? The unexpected wagon ride back to school from getting name cards? Perhaps you are a more casual fan, with vague memories of the warm feelings the book series conjured for you.

Whatever your memory serves up from the pages of Laura's books, you can easily imagine it happening in De Smet. Not only did the biggest chunk of the series take place here, it was the final stop for her parents, and for Mary, all of whom remained there, more or less, for the rest of their lives.

Laura never stopped missing De Smet, and the love for her first real hometown is evident in the way she wrote about it. As long as readers keep visiting every summer, that love lives on. You can still stand inside the very Surveyors' House Laura stayed in that first winter (and it's exactly as she described), wander over the family's homestead claim, and walk up and down Laura's Main Street. You can live your own Laura story.

Chapter 1
OVERVIEW of DE SMET

OUT OF ALL OF THE BOOKS in Laura Ingalls Wilder's series, fully half of them take place in one location: De Smet, South Dakota: *By the Shores of Silver Lake*, *The Long Winter*, *Little Town on the Prairie*, and *These Happy Golden Years*. (The posthumously published *The First Four Years* also takes place in De Smet.)

De Smet has plenty to entice you as a Laura Ingalls Wilder homesite: houses she and her family lived in, the land they homesteaded, not to mention artifacts and news clippings from their lives. Besides Mansfield, Missouri, where Laura lived from 1894 until her death in 1957, the De Smet homesite probably offers the most authentic artifacts from Laura's life.

Although formal categories don't exist, De Smet is considered a "major" Laura Ingalls Wilder homesite and is open year-round, though weekend activity is restricted to summer. A little bit of wandering reveals that you are indeed in Laura Ingalls Wilder country, from the road signs and storefronts to street names like Wilder Lane (get both references?) and Prairie Avenue. De Smet's elementary school is named after her, as is the highway that brings you into town. From the tiny downtown to the off-by-itself homestead to the cemetery south of town, De Smet emotes all Laura, all the time.

De Smet is the county seat of Kingsbury County, South Dakota, located at the junction of US 14 (east-west) and

Highway 25 (north-south) in the eastern part of the state. Like all other homesite locations, De Smet is a very small town—just over one square mile, similar to most of the towns in its vicinity. While pheasant hunting is a significant draw during the fall hunting season, Laura Ingalls Wilder tourism brings wagonloads of people into the town each summer. The population of De Smet hovers around 1,100, and it's a farming (corn, wheat, soybeans) and manufacturing community. The quarter-section that Charles Ingalls farmed, now open to the public as Ingalls Homestead, is just southeast of town, close enough but still too far for most to want to go on foot—unless you're walking home with Pa from your job with Miss Bell. Just watch out for the slough. (Yes, there is a Big Slough. More on that later.)

Please note: In her books, Laura referred often to "Main Street." It's where Pa's store building was, as well as such businesses as Fuller's Hardware and the Loftus Store. Today that street is known as Calumet Avenue. Whenever I mention Calumet Avenue, I am referring to the "Main Street" that is in Laura's books.

HOW LONG SHOULD A TRIP TO DE SMET BE?

The shortest trip to De Smet should last at least one full day, with an overnight at each end. For diehard fans, it's longer.

Despite the town's tiny size, its prevalence in the books means that there's quite a lot to do and see. In fact, several De Smet business owners have told me that visitors often leave wishing they had been able to stay longer. Ann Lesch, director of lodging and entertainment attraction Ingalls Homestead, frequently comes across travelers who stop by for an afternoon on their way somewhere else. By 5 PM they realize they want to stay longer, but by that time everything they wanted to do and see is starting to close— or there's no last-minute lodging available allowing them to extend their trip.

Don't be caught short. As a rule of thumb, schedule more time than you think you need.

THE BEST TIME TO GO

In *The Long Winter*, winter began in October and didn't end until May. The real De Smet follows a similar seasonal schedule. Much of the town is open year-round, as the area boasts an active fall hunting season and visitors trickle into town all year long for tours of the Laura Ingalls Wilder Historic Homes. But there is still a "season" when the most tourists descend on the town each year—roughly May through October.

De Smet is most crowded on July weekends, when the annual outdoor pageant is scheduled. For a quieter summer experience, try going in June or August, particularly mid-week, or even early September if you have that flexibility.

The Laura Ingalls Wilder Memorial Society, which runs tours through its authentic buildings related to the Ingalls and Wilder families — the Laura Ingalls Wilder Historic Homes — is open year-round, with limited hours in winter (no weekends). It's also closed on major holidays (but is open on July 4). Field trips are heavy in May.

Ingalls Homestead is the other main attraction in De Smet. It's outdoors, so it does not officially open until May (although you can call and email them year round). Each spring it welcomes as many as two thousand students for field trips starting in late April and throughout May. If you call ahead, I'm told, it's possible to join one of their visits (but only on school days, Monday through Friday). Tourist numbers increase toward the end of May when schools begin to let out, and then the summer season runs until school begins and the crowds taper off again.

It's important to keep in mind that many businesses close on Sundays. Ingalls Homestead is open seven days a week, as is the Laura Ingalls Wilder Memorial Society and its Historic Homes tours. But several restaurants are closed. The De Smet pageant, which brings the biggest populations of travelers to the town, *does* take place on Sunday evenings in July (in addition to Fridays and Saturdays), so some businesses will have special Sunday hours during pageant season.

WEATHER: WIND, SUN, AND STORMS

Remember Mrs. Brewster? Those prairie winds nearly drove her insane. It's true: De Smet can be extremely windy. Keep that in mind if you're a hat-wearer or simply have an aversion to wind (or dust).

While you are more likely than not to be greeted with days full of Dakota sunshine (remember your sunblock), it does rain occasionally. It's a farming community, so respect the locals and never complain about rain.

The "summer storms" Laura wrote about are also true to form for the area, typically showing up in the afternoon. Ingalls Homestead has addressed this weather tendency by building a storm shelter, which can be used by both visitors to the site and those who camp there overnight. But while these afternoon storms can be fierce, they usually do not last any more than 20 minutes. Don't panic and you'll be fine.

Chapter 2
GETTING THERE

DE SMET IS LOCATED IN EASTERN South Dakota, about 60 miles west of the Minnesota border.

One of the most important things to keep in mind if you're driving from the west (Mount Rushmore or the Black Hills) is that the time changes halfway across the state, which means you'll arrive in De Smet an hour later than you might have expected.

Also, even though trains feature heavily in Laura's stories and the train tracks run right through De Smet, these are no longer passenger trains. You cannot get to De Smet by train. (Iimagine if we *could?*)

To get to De Smet you have to either drive or use a combination of driving and flying.

FLYING

Sioux Falls. Sioux Falls, South Dakota, is the closest major (well, minorly major) airport to the area. Southeast of De Smet on Interstate 90, it's just under 100 miles away and the drive should take less than two hours.

The added bonus of flying into Sioux Falls is that it is almost equidistant between De Smet and Walnut Grove, Minnesota. Frankly, if you're going to De Smet, it's almost foolish not to add in a side trip to Walnut Grove; driving between the two is a very easy trip of less than two hours on the Laura Ingalls Wilder Memorial Highway (US Highway 14).

Minneapolis. Minneapolis is about a four-and-a-half-hour drive from De Smet, and that's a straight shot without stopping anywhere. However, it's worth considering as a destination airport. First, because the airport is so much bigger, fares can sometimes be cheaper than flying into Sioux Falls, which can make a difference when traveling with a family. Also, flying into Minnesota opens up the option for stops at other homesites: Pepin, Wisconsin, Laura's birthplace, just an hour and a half outside of the city; and Walnut Grove, Minnesota, right on the same highway as De Smet. If you have more time, you can also hit Burr Oak, Iowa, as well as Spring Valley, Minnesota. Laura lived in both places, though neither is mentioned in her books.

Car rental. If you're flying, there's no public transportation at all to De Smet, so renting a car is a must. Car rental in Sioux Falls is a little limited, because the airport isn't in a metropolis. Minneapolis will give you far more selection.

DRIVING

De Smet sits on US Highway 14, aka The Laura Ingalls Wilder Memorial Highway, in east-central South Dakota, 45 miles north of Interstate 90, 45 miles east of US Hwy 281, 60 miles from the Minnesota border, and a six- to seven-hour (give or take) eastward ride across the state from Mount Rushmore and the Black Hills. (The South Dakota interstate can be very windy, so both hands on the wheel.)

GENERAL GUIDANCE ON DIRECTIONS

From Sioux Falls airport (or from the south)

From the airport you can either drive west on the interstate and then turn north at US-81 or you can drive straight north on I-29 to Brookings, then head west on

Highway 14. Both will get you to De Smet in the same amount of time.

Going through Brookings is the most direct shot to De Smet—straight north and then straight west—so there is far smaller chance of getting lost. Also, restaurant options are more plentiful. Nick's Burgers is a nationally known legend, and there are wonderful specialty eateries popping up all the time. And of course, it's on the Laura Ingalls Wilder Historic Highway, US Highway 14.

Driving on the interstate, though, allows you to come into De Smet from the south, which is the same road that Laura, Almanzo, and Rose traveled when they left De Smet for Missouri in 1894, as described in *On the Way Home*. Taking that route also gives you a good idea of the landscape Laura and Almanzo drove through during their Sunday buggy rides.

From the east (Minnesota)

Going this way—taking US Highway 14 during the last stretch, at least—you're following the Ingalls family's route!

You'll find De Smet 60 miles into South Dakota from the Minnesota state line. The largest town you'll drive through coming this way is Brookings, which is right on US Highway 14 about 40 miles east of De Smet. Besides the previously mentioned reasons for driving through Brookings, it's a good-sized university town with pretty much anything you'd want, including hotels in case the lodging in De Smet is all sold out. (This happens.) There are also large grocery stores and a Walmart, and rumors are swirling about a Target opening. By the time you read this, there may be one!

From the west (western South Dakota and Mt. Rushmore area)

If you drive in from the west you will most likely be on Interstate 90. Take the exit for Mitchell and head north. Mitchell is also a decently sized town with a Walmart, grocery stores for necessities, and restaurants, so it's a good stop for stocking up. Plus—tell the outdoor enthusiasts in your group—it's got a Cabela's for outdoor and sporting goods. And if you're looking for a memorable tourist stop, the Corn Palace is a one-of-a-kind place. In 2024, the side wall of the palace incorporated gigantic corn-made murals of famous South Dakotans, including one of Laura. Check if it's still there if you plan to go.

If you end up driving from to De Smet from the west on US Highway 14, you'll go through Manchester, where Grace Ingalls Dow lived after marrying Nate Dow, and where Laura held down the claim with Mrs. McKee in *These Happy Golden Years*. (Manchester was, sadly, annihilated by a tornado in 2003 and has since become a ghost town. It was officially unincorporated the following year.)

Speed limits

The speed limit on the South Dakota interstate is 80; on other highways, like Highway 14, it's 65. If you're driving from Minnesota into South Dakota, keep in mind that the speed limit on Highway 14 increases from 55 to 65 once you cross the state line. (This is, admittedly, easier to adjust to than driving east, when the speed limit drops from 65 to 55 on Highway 14 once you cross into Minnesota. I have a $150 speeding ticket to prove it, and I'm not the only one.) Also, obey the speed limits in Kingsbury County—the county that includes De Smet—because they do ticket.

Maps and apps

Most of the driving in this part of South Dakota is straight-line driving, with lots of lefts and rights, easts and wests. Navigating will not be confusing. Different localities typically sprout water towers with the town's name emblazoned on them. It is very hard to get lost, as long as you know where you are.

Travel South Dakota is a stellar resource for vacationing in South Dakota. The website offers several maps for downloading or even snail-mailing. I know we're all used to GPS by now, but paper maps can be surprisingly helpful. If you find yourself driving and map-less, you can often find them at service stations or at one of the Interstate Information Centers along the highway.

DE SMET WEBSITES FOR TRIP PLANNING

In addition to information, most of these sites offer handy online maps to help you get around the small town of De Smet and identify everything worth seeing related to Laura Ingalls Wilder.

De Smet, SD (desmetsd.com)
The De Smet Development Corporation's website is geared toward tourists and offers the best local guidance about the town as well as a downloadable Community Guide. Its Laura Ingalls Wilder section is quite thorough.

City of De Smet, SD (cityofdesmet.com)
The City of De Smet website is for the benefit of De Smet's residents as opposed to tourists, but it does contain information visitors might find helpful.

Laura Ingalls Wilder Memorial Society (discoverlaura.org)
Discover Laura is the website of the Laura Ingalls Wilder Memorial Society, which runs the Historic House Tours

You'll find an online map on the website of the Laura Ingalls Wilder Memorial Society.

Ingalls Homestead (ingallshomestead.com)
Ingalls Homestead's website orients you to the land the Ingalls family homesteaded, which is open to visitors and self-guided tours.

De Smet Pageant (DeSmetPageant.org)
There's also useful visitor information on the website for De Smet's pageant.

You can also pick up paper maps in person; several places in town offer them.

More information on all of these are in **APPENDIX: RESOURCES**.)

Chapter 3
POINTS OF INTEREST
&
HOW TO FIND THEM

Like many of Laura's "little towns," De Smet is tiny and not difficult to navigate. The more ambitious among us can easily walk anywhere we'd like to go in the main part of town. But a car is recommended to get to a few outside-of-town attractions such as Ingalls Homestead, the De Smet Cemetery, and Laura and Almanzo's homestead claim.

U.S. Highway 14 runs east and west at the south end of town; the railroad tracks parallel this at the north end of town. SD Highway 25, running north and south, bisects the town (but it's one block west of Calumet Avenue).

Most businesses follow business hours, closing around 5 p.m., though some are open special hours on pageant weekends in July. (And—pro tip—parking is free. Everywhere. All the time.)

My single best suggestion is that before you embark on any exploration of De Smet, ask wherever you stop what's new this year. Every season brings new updates; the best way to find out is to ask.

To follow are the relevant points of interest in De Smet.

ARRIVING IN TOWN

City Hall

With the possible exception of checking in to your lodging, a good choice for your first stop in De Smet would be City Hall. There's a helpful visitors' center inside where you can ask questions, get recommendations on where to go, and find maps of the town.

It's located at the north end of town, across Calumet Avenue (Laura's "Main Street") from Maynard's Food Center, the only grocery store in town. It's open 9-5 (closed over lunch) Monday through Friday only. It's closed on weekends.

There is a Wilder Welcome Center in town that still exists, but Covid unfortunately hampered its staffing and funding so it is only open sporadically.

Several blocks east of Main Street is the Laura Ingalls Wilder Memorial Society. It also has served as the unofficial visitors' center for the town, because that's where travelers tend to go when they arrive in De Smet. Or after business hours, some will ask questions at the Oxbow, the first restaurant you see as you drive in.

The Laura Ingalls Wilder Memorial Society

The Laura Ingalls Wilder Memorial Society is the original organization dedicated to Laura Ingalls Wilder preservation in De Smet. It's three blocks east of Calumet Avenue on Olivet Avenue. The gift shop, which also functions as the headquarters for the Historic Homes tour, is open year-round except for major holidays, with longer hours in the summer season (and it is open on July 4th, Memorial Day, and Labor Day) and closed on weekends in the winter. Tours are offered at regular intervals every open day during the summer. Winter tours are more restrictive; call to find out what's offered if you'll be traveling between October and May. And keep in mind that school field trips tend to happen in May.

Make sure to set aside time to investigate the gift shop either before or after your tour. Mugs, books, water bottles, dishtowels, tea sets, china shepherdesses, jams and jellies, t-shirts, sweatshirts, prairie dresses, sunbonnets—so much to choose from!

Keep in mind that the tours have specific start times, so on busy summer days you may find that you have to book a slot for a little later in the day and come back. But everything in De Smet is so close, it's no trouble to check out a few other things while you're waiting. Or simply browse the gift shop.

The tour is slightly spread out, takes about two hours, and leads you through three places: The Surveyors' House, the First School of De Smet, and the Third Street House (more on these separately below). In addition to these three houses, your tour admission also grants you entry to the museum exhibit behind the gift shop (in the same building). The Memorial Society has a robust collection of Ingalls- and Wilder-related original artifacts. In recent years this area has expanded, offering extremely rich and detailed exhibits that will delight any serious Laura fan. Prepare to stay a while. Such exhibits are expected to be updated every couple of years.

The society has also been known to offer hands-on projects to the public such as crafts or other organized activities—sometimes in the Discover Laura Center (across the street from the gift shop) or in the adjacent picnic area. If your stay includes a weekend, be sure to find out what events might be going on while you're there.

The Surveyors' House (tours only)

Yes, this is the very same Surveyors' House where the Ingalls family spent the winter of 1879-1880 in *By the Shores of Silver Lake*. It is right next to the LIWMS headquarters and gift shop, but it has been moved from its original location next to Silver Lake. Standing inside, in the largest house twelve-year-old Laura had ever lived in, is magical.

The First School of De Smet (tours only)

Also relocated, this school was built in 1880 and attended by Laura and Carrie (and presided at one point by Eliza Jane Wilder) and is one of the newer permanent exhibits the Society has opened. Curators have dug down in layers of the wall to show the blackboard and even identify the chalk ledge. Inside you'll find tie-ins to Laura's time at the school, including the day she and Carrie had to walk home in the blizzard.

The Third Street House (tours only)

After *These Happy Golden Years* ended, Pa "proved up" on his homestead claim and in 1887 he built a house for him, Ma, Carrie, Grace, and eventually Mary on Third Street in town. You can't get in without a scheduled tour from the Laura Ingalls Wilder Memorial Society, but it's still nice to know the location, because it's not that far a walk from Calumet Avenue. (It's also two doors down from Prairie House Manor, a bed and breakfast that used to be the home of "Banker" Ruth, mentioned in the book series.) Besides touring the house, in the kitchen visitors can flip through enlarged newspaper clippings and other information detailing the Ingalls' stay in De Smet or inspect the many authentic Ingalls artifacts displayed in glass cases. (See a reference to this house in "Grandpa's Fiddle" by

Rose Wilder Lane, published in the William Anderson–edited *A Little House Reader.*)

It's worth noting that the Third Street House is quite a few blocks away from the gift shop, Surveyors' House, and First School of De Smet. Total distance is about a half-mile. Many people drive to the Third Street House from the Memorial Society headquarters after they have gone through the Surveyor's House and First School of De Smet, and they meet the tour guide there. That's fine, and I've done that. But having spent a lot of time in De Smet, I can say it's honestly not too far of a walk, especially on a lovely summer day when you could stop at Ward's or the De Smet Mercantile and Coffeehouse for an ice cream or dessert (or even lunch) on the way back. Ask about this first, so you can confirm you have time to walk; the guide may prefer that the entire tour arrive at the same time, in which case driving makes more sense.

Discover Laura Center

The Discover Laura Center, located across the street from the Memorial Society gift shop and Surveyors' House—where the tour begins—is an absolute treasure for small children. A one-room schoolhouse complete with desks and chalkboards, it's filled with all kinds of fun activities for kids, including pioneer clothing to dress up in, for boys as well as girls. Kids could easily be entertained for an hour, even two. Sometimes organized activities (butter-making, crafts) are offered there. It's also adjacent to a playground in the 4-H park, which includes a sheltered picnic area and cozy shaded benches as well as every parent's saving grace: restrooms.

Self-guided Tour in Downtown De Smet

The Memorial Society has created a self-guided tour for visitors who would like to know what they're looking at as they stroll through De Smet. It takes about an hour and only requires a map and your two feet. The tour centers on Calumet Avenue (Laura's "Main Street"), where signs installed on storefronts tell you that, for example, this was where Jake Hopp—of name card fame—started one of the town's newspapers. Or that you're standing in front of what used to be Fuller's Hardware, directly across the street from where Pa's store building stood during *The Long Winter*. Or the building where Laura sewed for Miss Bell. This is a wonderful tour making use of the reader's imagination and really brings Laura's town to life. You can almost see the dust from horses' hooves or the hitching posts they were tied to on the side of the street, or imagine Bill O'Dowd walking down the sidewalk with "Tay Pay" Pryor, kicking holes in each door's mosquito netting.

As of this writing the walking tour is being enhanced, improving signage and infrastructure on Calumet Avenue to make the tour even better. But don't worry, even if parts of it are under construction you'll still be able to see everything you need to.

Hazel L. Meyer Memorial Library

Like so much in the Land of Laura, De Smet's library is tiny but amazing. It is lined with all kinds of Laura-related artifacts, books, and documents. I could easily spend 30 minutes just walking around reading everything. (And I have.) The library is toward the north end of town, past the grocery store, on the east/right side of Main Street/Calumet Avenue—just south of the train tracks.

First Congregational Church

In *By the Shores of Silver Lake*, the Ingalls household hosts the first church service in the city of De Smet. Historically, this appears to be true. Later on services were held in the depot building at the north end of town (remember Ben's birthday party? more on that below!) until funds allowed the building of a Congregational Church in 1882, with Reverend Edward Brown presiding and Charles, Caroline, and Mary Ingalls listed as charter members. Billed as "the church that Pa built" because Charles Ingalls assisted in its construction, the De Smet Alliance Church, as it is now known, is on the corner of Second Street and Loftus Avenue. A bell purchased for the church in 1884 is still in use, but at the De Smet Community Church (formerly the United Church of Christ) building on US Highway 14.

The Loftus Store

Run by the Kruse family along with the adjoining Prairie Flowers florist, the Loftus Store—where Laura got Pa's suspenders during *The Long Winter*—is a sweet gift shop right on Calumet Avenue. (In the same block are the sites of Power's Tailor Shop, Bradley's Drugstore and Fuller's Hardware, though the stores are long gone.) The Loftus Store is well worth visiting for their unique Laura Ingalls Wilder–inspired gifts. And yes, they have suspenders!

Fr. Pierre Jean De Smet/Washington Park

De Smet is named after a missionary named Fr. Pierre Jean De Smet. There's a statue of him in Washington Park, toward the west side of town. Washington Park is a wonderful place to stretch little legs (and big ones, too). It's refreshingly shaded, with beautiful gardens, and includes a playground (look for the red structures) and restrooms.

The Depot Museum

Remember Ben Woodworth's birthday party in *Little Town on the Prairie*? He lived above the train depot. Rebuilt in the early twentieth century after a fire, the depot is functional today only as a museum. It's located at the north end of town and its collection, while not specifically Laura-centric, will please anyone interested in the area's history. From newspaperman Aubrey Sherwood's old typewriters and printing equipment to vintage clothing to railroad artifacts and displays of local wildlife, it's well worth a visit. Adjacent to the museum is the Harvey Dunn School, an homage to the famous South Dakota artist (and the nephew of Laura's sister Grace's husband, Nate Dow) in the school he attended as a child.

Although admission is free, donations are accepted (and encouraged—by me anyway).

De Smet City Pool

Don't forget you have an opportunity for respite from the scorching summer days. The De Smet City Pool opens in the afternoon and welcomes both adults and kids. It closes for lessons around dinnertime but reopens afterward and is available for night swimming on weeknights (including Friday). If an evening storm develops, though, they'll have to empty the pool—ask me how I know!

De Smet Event & Wellness Center

Located on the west side of town across the street from Washington Park, the De Smet Event & Wellness Center completed initial construction and was opened for business in 2015. It was built to serve both the town residents and seasonal visitors, with an eye toward giving tourists something to do in the evenings after everything else has closed. With an exercise center, a basketball court, a walking track, a reception and gathering area, and an indoor fireplace, it is an ideal spot for friends or families to visit during the day or gather in the evenings. It's open and staffed Monday through Friday, and a nominal fee is charged for use of the indoor gym equipment or basketball court. An outdoor patio area is also available.

From April through September on varying Sundays once a month the Center hosts a concert series that brings in national touring acts. They also offer theater shows. You'll find their calendar on the De Smet, SD website.

Another benefit the Center offers that is worth mentioning in the age of remote work is a professional work area. If you need to make calls or write a presentation, for example, the Center has space you can use for free.

JUST OUTSIDE OF TOWN

The Cottonwood Memorial Site

The Cottonwood Memorial Site is one of the first memorials to Laura Ingalls Wilder created in De Smet. On a corner of land that Charles Ingalls originally homesteaded, it's a gorgeous site surrounding the cottonwood trees that Pa allegedly planted in *By the Shores of Silver Lake*. It also includes a picturesque path up a hill to a memorial marker.

Although this memorial site borders the fee-based attraction known as Ingalls Homestead, a fence separates the two. (Barbed wire, unfortunately.) If you're already on Ingalls Homestead you can't legally enter the cottonwood site, and instead have to exit the property, then circle back around the road to the entrance. But it is worth seeing, and beautiful, so I suggest stopping there on your way into

Ingalls Homestead rather than being frustrated at being unable to enter later on.

Ingalls Homestead

Think of Dakota sunsets. Of Grace, lost among the violets. Of Laura rolling down the hill. Of Ma, bending over the chickens to check that they were safe. This all happened on Ingalls Homestead.

Every visitor leaves De Smet in love with Ingalls Homestead. As a Laura Ingalls Wilder fan, simply standing on the land that Charles Ingalls homesteaded in the 1880s and imagining Laura walking over the very hill on which I'm standing is enough to give me chills. Many fans say— and I'm one of them—that Ingalls Homestead is one of those places where you really "feel" Laura. For a panoramic view of it all, you can climb a fire tower on the property, and maybe see all the way to the Wessington Hills.

As a parent, I love Ingalls Homestead for an additional reason: the space.

If you have small children, this is your place. No chasing toddlers down hallways or out doors or holding onto them tightly so they won't break valuables. You can just put your kids down and let them run free. (And even though it's big, it's not so big that you would lose your kids in, say, a buffalo wallow.) It's also worth noting that even if Laura fandom isn't a father's thing, he will at least appreciate the break from kid-wrangling and the freedom that comes with that. In fact, the Homestead is probably the most interesting attraction to non-fans, especially if they have even a passing interest in history or American pioneering.

Best of all, your admission ticket to Ingalls Homestead is good not just for the day you buy it, but for your entire visit to De Smet. You can come back again and again.

Ingalls Homestead is owned by the Sullivan family and has been in operation in its current incarnation—evolving further every year—since the late 1990s. The exact same quarter section that Charles Ingalls homesteaded in the 1880s, just southeast of De Smet (and on the other side of the real Big Slough), is wide open and available for walking, running, playing, camping, or just drinking in the prairie vistas.

Admission covers everyone over age four (four and under is free). You may purchase a water bottle if you find yourself staying too long under that Dakota sun, and you are of course welcome to shop the gift store, but other than that, the admission fee gets you everything you need. It's fully family-friendly. Kids can duck inside a dugout, make button-string crafts, ride miniature horses, wash clothes on a washboard, take a turn at an antique sewing machine, grind wheat in a coffee grinder, pump water from the ground, twist hay into sticks, make corncob dolls like Susan (it wasn't her fault she was only a corncob), and ride a horse-drawn covered wagon across the prairie to join in a genuine 1880s schoolhouse lesson.

For that matter, so can adults. "For the record," one traveler tells me, "an adult on a solo trip feels just as at home simply breathing the air." Ingalls Homestead is truly a multi-generational destination. Because Laura Ingalls Wilder wrote her books for children, the Sullivans, parents of four children themselves, wanted to create an environment where kids could feel welcome—where the attitude is always "please touch." The Homestead's patriarch, Tim Sullivan, says the place is a draw for all ages, "from grandparents to grandchildren. Families recall past memories and make new ones."

Then there are the kittens. Every year new kittens roam the Homestead, and believe me when I tell you a child of a certain age can easily spend *hours* with the kittens.

Bottom line: if the kids have fun, everyone has fun. Everything is designed primarily for the enjoyment of children. On the wagon ride across the prairie to the schoolhouse, young passengers are offered a chance to drive the horses. Then they get to dress up in bonnets and hats for the schoolhouse lesson.

When to go? If you have the choice to visit Ingalls Homestead in the morning or the afternoon, opt for the afternoon, because it's open after the last Historic House tours end back in town at the Laura Ingalls Wilder Memorial Society.

However, if it's intensely hot outside, you might want to visit the Historic Houses in the afternoon when the sun is at its strongest.

When you are planning, I would set aside—yes, you're reading this right—three hours for Ingalls Homestead. Possibly even four. People who go there have a hard time leaving. It's true. Go visit there and tell me you don't feel the same.

And remember that if you decide to, say, head back to the homestead in the morning before leaving town, perhaps for one last look at that gorgeous prairie or so your kids can have 10 more minutes of kitten cuddling, just bring your admission sticker. Again, it's good for your whole visit, not just the day you bought it.

The De Smet Cemetery

The cemetery where the entire Ingalls family (except for Laura) is buried is located south of town. Take US Highway 14 west, and take a left to turn south onto Prairie Avenue. Prairie Avenue ends one mile south; turn right. The cemetery will be ahead of you on the left. The Ingalls graves are on the far south side of the cemetery, right on the edge near the gravel road surrounding it. But it's worth it to get out of your car for a while to look around. Walking among the graves, you'll see lots of names right out of the book series, like Boast, Gilbert, and Brown for starters. Go ahead and test yourself; see how many you can find.

The Ingalls graves are protected by a chain, which is understandable given the traffic. But it does make the area rather unsightly.

Grace Ingalls Dow's grave is not in the Ingalls family plot; it's further west, a little down the hill (just follow the sidewalk; it's the only sidewalk there) behind the rest of her family's plots, next to her husband, Nate Dow.

As you're leaving the cemetery, there is a lovely memorial site off to the right established to remember De Smet residents who were killed in accidents. It's a calm, peaceful spot to wander through or sit and take a moment to yourself.

The Big Slough

Remember the Big Slough? Of course you do. It's real. "Slough" is pronounced SLOO, and De Smet has quite a few of them. But the "big" one is between town and Ingalls Homestead; look off to the right when you're driving from town and you'll see its tall grasses.

Silver Lake and the Laura Ingalls Wilder Wilderness Trail

Silver Lake is arguably the most recognizable location in all of De Smet, simply by virtue of its inclusion in the title of a book. In an ideal world, getting to it would be as easy as getting to Plum Creek in Walnut Grove.

But Silver Lake is not nearly as accessible as Plum Creek. Some of that is due to the nature of the land. The word you might have heard on the street is that Silver Lake was drained due to mosquitoes (remember the trouble the Ingalls family had with them in *By the Shores of Silver Lake*?), or to create farmland. It's true that the lake dried out at least twice in the twentieth century. In the past few decades the Silver Lake slough has been refilling and is now marked with a sign on US Highway 14 just east of town. It's a very marshy area, not much different than the sloughs around it.

The city of De Smet established the **Laura Ingalls Wilder Wilderness Trail** to help visitors see the lake as Laura did, or as close as you can get to that in the 21st century. It begins at the intersection of Lyle Avenue and 4th Street, where a walking path leads the way to the "shore" of Silver Lake.

A multi-year, state-supported project to extend the trail all the way to US Highway 14 and eventually add a lookout tower is underway. Ask about its progress while you're in town. It's an ambitious project with significant support, but it also requires significant funding.

FURTHER AFIELD

Laura and Almanzo's Homestead

This site is marked not just because Laura and Almanzo lived here, but because it's the birthplace of their daughter, Rose Wilder Lane. It's located on Highway 25 about a mile and a half north of town, on the left. There are no buildings surviving and the site is privately owned and not open to the public, but there's a heck of a view.

In 2024 the site was in the news under threats that it was going to be developed as a gravel mine. Although it did seem to be "saved" for the time being, its future is unclear.

Almanzo Wilder's Tree Claim

Another mile further north of town on Highway 25 you'll find the local airport (Wilder Airport) on the left. This was the second homestead that Almanzo Wilder developed as a tree claim—the "little gray home in the west"—and where the Wilders' house burned down. Only a few remnant trees are seen near the highway.

Lake Thompson

Ah, remember those Sunday drives to and around Lake Henry and Lake Thompson in *These Happy Golden Years*? Located 10 miles from De Smet, today's Lake Thompson is absolutely huge—it's the second-largest natural lake in South Dakota. It's officially located in the town of Lake Preston. Drive 4 miles east of De Smet on Highway 14 and 6 miles south to get to the park and docks.

Spirit Lake

Another of Laura and Almanzo's Sunday destinations, the "beautiful and wild" Spirit Lake on the north side of De Smet can still be described that way today. Take 25 north about 10 miles, then turn left for 12 more miles, and you'll find Spirit Lake on the right.

OTHER EVENTS

Laura Ingalls Wilder is not the only game in town. Two notable non-Laura events happen each summer in De Smet.

Old Settler's Days

Every second weekend of June, De Smet hosts its Old Settler's Days, which Laura herself attended back in the 1930s.

Harvey Dunn Memorial Society Plein Air Event

Harvey Dunn was not only a renowned South Dakota artist, he was also the nephew of Nate Dow, who married Laura's sister Grace. Dunn was born in Manchester—where Laura held down the claim with Mrs. McKee in *These Happy Golden Years*—in 1884, the year before Laura and Almanzo married. He was esteemed particularly for his renditions of the Dakota prairie scenes he knew so well. Run by the Harvey Dunn Memorial Society, The Plein Air Event is a marvelous artistic festival that takes place over the second weekend of August and features artists of all levels painting in the "open air" on the prairie. Visitors can socialize in the evenings over hors d'oeuvres and sandwiches. Paintings created over the weekend are put on display Sunday afternoon and offered for sale.

CHURCHES

Traveling on a Sunday? Families of all Christian denominations will find welcoming Lutheran, Congregational, Catholic, and Methodist services offered in the area, most of them on the west side of town. All are listed on the city of De Smet's website.

Chapter 4
THE DE SMET PAGEANT

DE SMET'S PAGEANT takes place during three weekends in July on Friday, Saturday, and Sunday nights. It's a play performed by locals on an outdoor stage in a field adjacent to Ingalls Homestead and the Cottonwood Memorial Site.

The pageant used to begin at 9 p.m., but in true family-friendly fashion, the start time was recently changed to 8 p.m. to accommodate families who might need to drive out of town after it's over. (In-town lodging tends to fill up on pageant weekends.) The pageant is usually over by 10 p.m.

Pro tip: Don't bother comparing De Smet's pageant to Walnut Grove's. Walnut Grove takes their pageant very seriously, and it shows. The fact that they have reserved seating and advance ticketing is a good indication of that.

In comparison, De Smet's pageant is more relaxed. It isn't necessary to buy tickets in advance; there is always room for everyone. "I've never turned anyone away," Tim Sullivan of Ingalls Homestead, who is on the pageant board, tells me. Seating runs up a low hill from the stage area, on backless benches arranged on the grass. But you can bring your own chairs and blankets for seating between the benches.

Concessions are available, selling hot dogs, candy, popcorn, soda/pop, and iced tea, and sometimes meals such as BBQ sandwiches are offered by various community groups. (I've even seen "Long Winter Snow Cones.") Lately local food trucks have also been around on pageant night.

You are welcome to bring your own picnic (and take care of your own trash), though keep in mind that supporting local sales help to keep the pageant going, so do buy what you can. (Although staff of Ingalls Homestead and the Laura Ingalls Wilder Memorial Society are on the pageant board and participate in its production, neither is affiliated financially with the pageant, which has its own budget.)

For kids waiting around for the pageant to begin, there's plenty of fun to keep them from getting antsy. Kids (and adults of course!) can ride for free in a horse-drawn open wagon around the pageant grounds. The Whatnot Shop is also on hand, selling books, prairie-inspired trinkets, bonnets, and T-shirts. Again, profits benefit the pageant itself, not Ingalls Homestead or the Laura Ingalls Wilder Memorial Society.

Although in the past the pageant has experimented with focusing on particular books, these days it tells "Laura's Dakota Stories" through the stage, following Laura's life from her move to De Smet at age 12 through meeting and marrying Almanzo Wilder at age 18. Presented as a trilogy of stories—one each year—the stage productions are told from the perspective of Laura and her journalist daughter, Rose Wilder Lane, who was instrumental to the process of writing and editing the book series.

A few pageant points to keep in mind:

Bring cash. Admission is cash-only if you're buying at the gate. You drive into the pageant site from an access road between Ingalls Homestead and Highway 14. Attendants will direct your car, and they accept only cash. If you want to pay by credit or debit card you can do so at the Ingalls Homestead gift store, which is open until 8 p.m. on pageant nights (7 p.m. normally). As with everything else, prices creep up year by year, so for specifics check online.

Admission for kids 6-12 is cheaper than adults', and under 5 is free. Parking is also free.

Bring a jacket. No matter how hot it is during the day, it almost always cools off significantly at night, often quite suddenly. When it cools off, it cools off fast.

Protect against mosquitoes. As mentioned previously, Big Slough + outdoors + nighttime = a mosquito festival. The grounds are sprayed for mosquitoes during pageant season, and bug spray is often provided and offered to visitors. But be on the safe side and bring your own, and make sure everyone's dressed in long pants and long sleeves for additional protection.

Chapter 5
LODGING

IN DE SMET, you can sleep under the twinkling (or winking) prairie stars if you like (just don't forget the mosquito spray). You can even stay in a covered wagon. For the more modern travelers among us, your lodging options include a traditional hotel, a smaller motel, bed and breakfasts, or a bunkhouse. All roofed lodging has free wireless for guests. Reviews of almost all options listed in this section are available online, which I encourage you to consult.

Where you stay is dependent on your tastes, plus when you're going, whom you're traveling with, how old your traveling companions are, and how long you plan to be in town.

Reservations recommended

Should you reserve lodging in advance? If you're planning to be in De Smet in July during a weekend when the pageant is taking place, or if you want to reserve wildly popular lodging like a covered wagon on Ingalls Homestead, the answer is a resounding YES—and do so as early as possible.

How early is early? Ingalls Homestead tells me they begin to field calls for the summer reservations around Christmas. Yes, six months in advance. (Years ago I myself tried to make a reservation in March at Prairie House Manor for one of two weekends in July—the horror. Of course both weekends were fully booked. Learn from my mistake.)

If camping is your thing, it's still wise to make reservations, especially if you need hookups. If you don't need hookups, there is plenty of space.

What are lodging prices like?

De Smet may be a tiny town in South Dakota, but because lodging is so limited there, during high season—that is, the summer—you won't find prices to be much lower than the average price you'd find elsewhere. Bottom line: don't expect discounts during the summer. The cheapest non-camping prices you'll find are the rustic lodging options on Ingalls Homestead; the most expensive can be found in family suites at Prairie House Manor or Heritage House Bed and Breakfast. In general your room rates include free wireless.

LODGING IN DE SMET

Cottage Inn

The Cottage Inn is "clean, basic, economy lodging in De Smet" according to one online review, and that's pretty much on the mark. With forty rooms spread out over several buildings, the Cottage Inn is larger than it looks. It's also more of a motel than a hotel, located right on Highway 14 and less expensive than the Super Deluxe Inn. The motel is run by the Myers family, who also own The Oxbow restaurant across the highway. They've had these businesses for two generations.

Super Deluxe Inn

The Super Deluxe Inn is the one mainstream, chain-style hotel in De Smet. Located right on US Highway 14 and close to the intersection at Highway 25, it used to be a Super 8 and features 37 rooms for the most private, anonymous accommodations in town. An indoor pool is available to guests, as well as free continental breakfast.

Prairie House Manor

Remember Banker Ruth, who bought the last bag of flour in town in *The Long Winter*? His former residence, just one block off Calumet Avenue, has been a bed and breakfast for twenty-five years. If you have kids and you're not a covered-wagon kind of vacationer, Prairie House Manor should be your first choice. The Todd family, originally from New Jersey, took it over from the Cheney family and ran it for fifteen years before it was sold in 2022 to Eric Fairchild and Rob Mann, who relocated from Colorado to oversee the establishment.

Prairie House Manor is ideal for singles or families, with rooms ranging from large to small, two on the ground floor and the rest upstairs. Two of the rooms have sun porches. As with any bed and breakfast, you have to be flexible about bathroom layout (although all rooms have their own bathrooms) and the general idiosyncrasies of this type of lodging. It's not a hotel and doesn't try to be. The living room and enclosed front porch are always open to current guests, and their layout encourages visiting. On the porch are kids' toys—many of them vintage from the 1970s and '80s.

Heritage House Bed and Breakfast

You can't get closer to downtown than this. It's right on Calumet Avenue (again, Laura's Main Street) and has a direct Ingalls connection: it's located in the bank where Caroline and Mary did their banking, and it's across the street from the former location of Pa's store building in town (the first one he built, not the house the family lived in later on Third Street, after the time of *These Happy Golden Years*). It has four rooms—including one three-room suite with a loft, great for families—all with private baths. Breakfast is, of course, included.

If you are traveling with multiple generations, Heritage House is an ideal choice for the older members of your party who may prefer to leave the camping or covered-wagon lodging to the younger folks.

Do keep in mind, again, the differences between staying at a bed and breakfast vs. more mainstream lodging. Besides the personal connection with the proprietors, which can seem odd if you're used to traveling in anonymity, such lodging is typically located in older buildings and often involves stairs rather than elevators, so it's not ideal for those who need accessibility. Some people love this atmosphere, but if you value total privacy and solitude, you will probably be happier in more standard lodging like the Super Deluxe Inn or the Cottage Inn.

Ingalls Homestead (for camping and rustic living)

Ingalls Homestead features four options for lodging, all rustic: tent camping (no hookups), RV camping (with hookups), covered wagons, and a bunkhouse. Both the bunkhouse and the wagons require you to provide your own linens. The bunkhouse is the most "modern," with sleeping room for six, a microwave, and a small refrigerator.

Covered wagons include electricity and not much else, but they sure are fun. One of them has a permanent light fixture, but the others have only outdoor outlets and a heavy-duty drop cord that runs into the wagon, so bring your flashlights and lanterns. The largest wagons have room for two adults and three small children to sleep. The other two are intended for three people, and small people at that.

Discuss with your reservationist which wagon(s) would work best for your family. Pro tip: If you have your heart set on a covered wagon and your dates are flexible, try a Tuesday or a Wednesday night in June or August.

All overnight visitors at Ingalls Homestead have access to campground-style restrooms and showers.

Washington Park (for camping)

Remember in *By the Shores of Silver Lake*, the Ingalls family finds out the town is named De Smet? It's named after Fr. Pierre Jean De Smet, and you can find a statue of this French namesake in Washington Park on the west side of town.

Washington Park is a large, lovely piece of *shaded* (emphasis mine), landscaped greenery perfect for taking a breather. It houses a playground (curly slide, climbing wall, etc.), horseshoe pits, and a sand volleyball court. Camping is offered alongside it (extra charge for electricity) for both tents and RVs; there are a very limited number of RV electrical hookups with 20 AMPs that are first-come, first-served.

Also important to note about Washington Park: restrooms and showers are available.

The Spot (for camping)

This RV park is located east of town on US Highway 14, between Ingalls Homestead and the town.

Vacation Rentals

A few Airbnb or VRBO rentals have been popping up in De Smet of late, so it pays to include them in your search.

LODGING OUTSIDE DE SMET

It's possible that by the time you are making your reservations, everywhere you'd like to stay in De Smet is booked. If you're shut out completely, there are other options.

Brookings

Brookings (mentioned in the books!) is only 45 minutes east of De Smet—which means 45 minutes closer to Walnut Grove, if you're going that way—and it's got all the amenities De Smet lacks, as well as a few additional attractions including a hands-on children's museum with a farming and weather-related play area that distinguishes it from similar museums in other regions; an art museum on the campus of South Dakota State University (including Harvey Dunn paintings); and the South Dakota Agricultural Heritage Museum.

However, keep in mind that even Brookings can get terribly busy in summer. If you're trying to get a same-day reservation, you may well be shut out. It's a popular stop for truckers and there are several events—such as its annual Art Festival in July—that invite large crowds at various times.

Arlington

Arlington is about 25 minutes east of De Smet, between De Smet and Brookings. The Arlington Inn used to be a Super 8 and sees a lot of repeat business. It also is within walking distance of the 1481 Grille, a well-reviewed restaurant that's open seven days a week.

Huron

Huron (mentioned in the books!) is about 35 miles to the west—on the way to the Black Hills and Mount Rushmore—and features four decent-sized hotels (and is famous for being the home of the World's Largest Pheasant). It also has an annual event to plan around, the late-summer South Dakota State Fair, which uses up all of the lodging in town.

Lake Thompson Recreation Area

The shore of Lake Thompson (*really* mentioned in the books) features a state park that's about a 10-mile drive from De Smet—4 miles east, then 6 south—in the town of Lake Preston. Yes, it's *that* Lake Thompson, notable not only as a frequent destination of nineteenth-century buggy rides but also for being the second-largest natural lake in the state. Campers have their choice of over 100 sites, and there are also a few cabins. The reservations system is very organized, depending on what your camping set-up requires. It does fill up early, and you can't reserve until 90 days before your stay. If you're a boater (or you're married to one), bring the boat.

North Shore Lodging and Campground

This camping/cabin area is near Lake Thompson State Park and used to house a (sadly missed) restaurant right on the lake shore. Now it offers rental of a lodge that sleeps up to twenty (think family reunions), plus a cabin that sleeps four, as well as campsites.

Please note: No boat rentals are available on Lake Thompson.

Other options

Other lodging options exist, depending on where you're traveling from and to. **Mitchell** is about 70 miles southwest, right on I-90 on the way to the Black Hills. **Watertown** is about 60 miles northeast (on 25) and makes sense if you're driving north; it also boasts the only Target in the area (though Brookings may have one by the time you read this).

Final lodging notes

If you're used to city standards, you may have to relax your expectations a little bit. Tourism is a huge chunk of De Smet's economy, but it's concentrated in one part of the year. As a result cancellation policies may be stricter than you would find at other locales.

In my experience the locals, especially the business owners who cater to tourists, are lovely to deal with and ready to help whenever and wherever they can. But that, of course, goes both ways. There's a small-town friendliness in De Smet. Embrace it and reciprocate it, and your De Smet experience can be happy, and golden.

Chapter 6
FOOD & DINING

I'LL BE HONEST: To me the most challenging part of traveling in the Land of Laura is the food. Then again, it all depends on what your eating habits are. I don't eat fast food and limit it with my children, so the fact that one of the main restaurants for a long time in De Smet was a Dairy Queen wasn't helpful to my family.

Likewise, you may have to relax your expectations when it comes to what restaurants are able to offer. Menus may not have gluten-free items or microgreen salads, and powdered creamer and margarine can often be found in place of real dairy. But on the flip side, when the food is good, it is usually homemade—and it is excellent.

Whether you're packing a cooler with ice or simply want a place to replenish granola bars, with kids in tow you'll want to know where to find the grocery store. In De Smet, there's only one. It's called Maynard's Food Center, and it's located on the north end of Calumet Avenue, just past the post office. Keep in mind, though, that it might close earlier than you are used to.

I will not be providing hours of operation for any of the restaurants. Changing ownership and other factors make it difficult to keep up with the fluctuating hours of operation, even for the locals. So I'll make just a couple of recommendations.

1. Call or check online first. Many restaurants are not open on Sunday, and some have seasonal hours.

2. Check the newspaper. I'm serious. The *Kingsbury Journal* can be your source for the most up-to-date information in town. (You can even subscribe to the electronic edition in advance: $50 for a year.)

3. If you're traveling from out of town and have confirmed where you're going to eat, consider checking the menu online first so you can have a leg up when you arrive after a long drive.

Important note: the information in this chapter is current as of 2025. But with the restaurant industry being as tumultuous as it is, anything can change. **Please verify everything before you make plans.**

DINING IN DE SMET

Dairy Queen/Subway

Unfortunately for those who like ice cream, as of 2025 the Dairy Queen in De Smet has closed. I'm keeping it listed in case it starts back up again.

Ward's Store & Bakery

A coffee bar that's open for breakfast and lunch, Ward's is one of my favorite places in De Smet. It's located in a building that once housed the De Smet Opera House, which was built in 1886—yes, while newly-married Laura lived there. Look up while you're inside, and you'll see the original tin ceiling. We can easily imagine that the Ingalls and Wilder families went there at some point. Over time it changed hands as a bank and as a JC Penney department store before becoming Ward's in the 1950s. (For more on the opera house, read John Miller's excellent *Laura Ingalls Wilder's Little Town*, a comprehensive history of De Smet in a Laura Ingalls Wilder context, or flip the restaurant's menu over—the story's repeated there, too.)

Ward's currently functions as a restaurant, gift shop, bakery, art gallery, coffee shop, clothing store, cell phone accessories store, and overall community center of sorts. You'll find members of the De Smet community around the tables at lunchtime or in and out for coffee, lemonade, slushies, or pastries throughout the day. It's strewn with Formica tables that would elsewhere be called charmingly retro; here they're just the tables (often pulled from the basements of longtime De Smet residents).

Ward's is open year-round, breakfast and lunch only, although during pageant weekends in the summer they sometimes stay open for special pageant dinners, including kids' meals or even outside grilling. Breakfast items are pretty straightforward—eggs, biscuits, bacon, coffee, and bakery items. All baked goods are homemade and scrumptious.

Lunchtime usually features a daily special, which is available as supplies last, although the grill does close at a certain time. (I talked to a traveler recently whose family was turned away for lunch at 1:45.) There's a high chair available for small children. The food is usually homemade and excellent—during one visit my sandwich was served on a pretzel roll—and although a deep fryer is available, the menu doesn't rely on deep-fried foods.

Sadly, Ward's is not open on Sundays. Everyone needs a break sometime! For Sunday breakfast in town, go to the Oxbow.

De Smet Mercantile and Coffeehouse

Happily, even with the closing of Dairy Queen, there is still an ice cream option in town, the De Smet Mercantile and Coffeehouse. Opened in 2021 and housed with a kid-oriented gift shop, beyond ice cream it offers coffee drinks, tasty sandwiches, and some baked goods.

The Oxbow

The Oxbow is a charming staple restaurant run by the Myers family and has been the most consistently open restaurant in De Smet. Open at 6 a.m., it's a great choice for breakfast. Closing hours vary depending on the day. The food it offers can easily be referred to as "home-style." It has decent desserts as well as ice cream, and it's also one of the only places in town that offers a salad bar, although the salad bar can be limited both in variety and hours of availability. Check the restaurant's Facebook page for consistent daily specials. The Oxbow is centrally located near the intersection of Highways 14 and 25 and is easily visible to passersby. Since it is so accessible and one of the only restaurants open on Sunday, on summer weekends, particularly pageant weekends, it can get pretty busy. On Sundays they usually have a brunch buffet.

Kingsbury County Country Club and Golf Course (currently Prairie Fire Bar and Grill)

Warning: the info in this section could change. For now I'll cautiously share that after a few years of closure, as of 2025 I'm tentatively hopeful that the new restaurant that opened at the Kingsbury County Country Club, Prairie Fire Bar and Grill, will be around for some time. This restaurant was my favorite for years but closed during the pandemic.

This restaurant isn't in the main part of town, but it takes 5 minutes to get there, if that. As its name implies, it is on the edge of the county's golf course. To get there, drive west on Highway 14 as if you're going out of town, then turn south (left) on Prairie Avenue, the same way you'd drive to the De Smet Cemetery. (You'll know the street because it's also directly opposite the water tower with "De Smet" emblazoned on it.) The second left off Prairie Avenue, less than a half-mile down the road, is 7th Street. Take it and you'll drive directly into the parking lot.

I haven't eaten at the current incarnation, but in the past it has featured steaks, seafood, chicken, burgers, sandwiches and all the side dishes; it also has a decent salad bar. Weekends have featured prime rib. I've tried a few different dishes there under various owners and the food has always been quite good, though on the more expensive side when you take all of the other area restaurants into consideration. There's also a full bar.

Every time I have been to De Smet during high-season, summer weekends, this restaurant has never been open on Sundays. However, because it's under new ownership, that schedule is definitely worth verifying.

The Dugout

This restaurant and bar (cute name, right?) is located on Calumet Avenue between Ward's and the post office. It's only open in the evenings, and not on Sundays. It's well known for its prime rib and great burgers. If you have only adults in your party, it could be a good choice.

Restaurant on Third Street

This restaurant has been known as Grumpy's, The Third Street Bar and Grille, the Hitchin' Post, and others. At the moment it's Half-Pint Steaks and Spirits. Whatever it's called, it's usually open, and usually pretty good. It has a full bar. It's got a memorable location—on Third Street just down the block from the house Charles Ingalls built and Prairie House Manor—between Calumet Avenue and Highway 25.

Wheaties

Wheaties, on Calumet Avenue across from Maynard's Food Center, is a dive. That's not an insult. The owner happily claims that moniker. It's also the home of the best burger in Kingsbury County. Seriously, it's won the award. Open hours are not consistent, but it's (generally) open for lunch and (generally) open for dinner. It's cash-only, and there's an ATM inside.

Wheaties also claims the category of casino, because it includes gambling machines. It's one of the few places that is open (generally) on Sundays.

Because it's a bar, and a self-described "dive bar" at that, I'm not going to encourage it for kids, but you can always get the food to go.

Gas stations—pizza and some sandwiches

Two gas stations in town, the Main Stop and the Cowboy Country Store, sell pizza. The Cowboy Country Store also sells chicken, burgers, and hot sandwiches. Both are across from the Oxbow at the corner of Calumet Avenue and Highway 14. Tables are available for sitting as well.

DINING OUTSIDE OF DE SMET

Because dining in De Smet is a bit limited, it can be worth leaving town for the evening meal, or on Sundays.

Lake Preston Cafe
Lake Preston SD
10-minute drive
This is on Main Street in Lake Preston (on the south side of US 14) and used to be J & M Café. Currently it's

open for breakfast, lunch, and dinner six days a week—just breakfast and lunch on Sundays—and it stays open late on Friday and Saturday nights.

1481 Grille
Arlington SD
25-minute drive
This restaurant named for the intersection of Highway 14 and 81 is worth the drive. The menu is extensive and consistently good, and prices are reasonable. It's open only for dinner, and until quite late. It also has a full bar. (If craft beer is your thing, this is where you want to eat.)

Cabaret Steakhouse and Lounge
120 Main St.
Carthage SD
30–35-minute drive
Carthage is 25 miles southwest of De Smet and can be reached either on the way north from I-90 or driving south out of town. Carthage is notable as being one of the locations where the movie "Into the Wild" was filmed. (The movie was based on a book by Jon Krakauer, about the life of Chris McCandless, who lived in Carthage for a time before heading to the wilderness of Alaska, where he perished.)

A FEW FINAL NOTES ON FOOD

Expect simplicity. While the homemade food is usually delicious, people with food sensitivities or strict diets (like vegans or gluten-free eaters) may have a tougher time than they would in a more metro area. If you are concerned with what you or your kids eat, or want access to food at any time, pack a cooler, load it up in Brookings, Huron, or Mitchell, and expect to frequent the grocery store.

New Facebook resource: There is a Facebook page called "What's Cooking in Kingsbury County." (De Smet is the county seat of Kingsbury County.) On it, area restaurants post their specials or any other food or restaurant news, usually with photos. If you have a trip to De Smet coming up, I recommend checking it out.

Look for pageant schedules. On pageant nights, different meals are likely available. Check for flyers around town to see what the offerings might be.

Remember Sunday closures. As of this writing only two restaurants in and around De Smet are open on Sunday: the Oxbow and the Lake Preston Café in Lake Preston (plus, occasionally, Wheaties of burger fame). But you never know when that could change, which brings me to …

Verify, verify, verify. Closures happen way more often than we'd like, so always verify when (and whether) the restaurant is open.

Bring cash. You'll thank me later.

Chapter 7
BUDGETING YOUR TRIP

DE SMET IS ONE OF THOSE GREAT destinations that
doesn't cost a whole lot of money, which is why it's so ideal
for the family. I recommend bringing cash. Many places
take credit cards in the land of Laura Ingalls Wilder, but far
more places than you'd expect do not. Make sure you have
cash on hand for those times. There are three ATMs in
town, one at The Main Stop gas station, which is only
accessible when the gas station is open, one in Wheaties
Bar and Grill (ditto) and one at the Dakotaland Federal
Credit Union, available 24/7 next to the drive-up window.
The two not in Wheaties are essentially across the street
from one another on Highway 14.

Because locals have told me it's the number-one
question they get asked, I'll reiterate that parking is free.
Everywhere. Whether you're at the Discover Laura Center,
Ward's, Ingalls Homestead, or the pageant site, no matter
where you are in De Smet or its vicinity, you never, ever
have to pay for parking. Great, isn't it?

WHAT YOU'LL PAY FOR

Besides your lodging and meals, there are only a few
extra items to budget for: admission and gift-shop items.
Admission fees are similar across all De Smet attractions.
You'll pay admission at the Laura Ingalls Wilder Memorial
Society for tours and the museum exhibit, at the Wilder

Pageant for that night's performance, and at Ingalls Homestead.

Remember that your Ingalls Homestead admission is good for your entire visit, no matter how many times you return. And the only time you're asked for money is at the "gate." Everything else—wagon rides, crafts, horseback rides—is included in your admission.

Gift shop items and donations

Of course, you don't have to shop in the gift shop at Ingalls Homestead, or at the Laura Ingalls Wilder Memorial Society, or in the Loftus Store, or in the Whatnot Shop at the pageant site. But particularly with the nonprofits, gift shop sales are what keep these places going. And they all offer something a little different—if you've seen one gift shop, you have not necessarily seen them all.

The Laura Ingalls Wilder Memorial Society also has a donor program with tiered levels for various projects they need to fund (such as repairing the foundation of the Surveyors' House and the siding and windows of the Third Street House). Check their website for current details.

Chapter 8
ITINERARIES

WHEN PLANNING A TRIP to De Smet—or anywhere—it helps to know how long things take. Here's a general idea of the minimum length of time to expect to spend on De Smet attractions:

Laura Ingalls Wilder Memorial Society tour: 2 hours

Museum exhibit: 1–2 hours

Self-guided walking tour of De Smet: 1 hour

Ingalls Homestead visit: 2–4 hours (with a possible second or even third visit)

Trip to cemetery: 1 hour (including drive time and walking around)

Time to drive to Rose's birthplace north of town, take a commemorative photo, and drive back: 15-20 minutes

Drive time to Lake Thompson: 10 minutes

Pageant length: two hours (ends by 10 p.m.)

Use these sample itineraries below to get to know De Smet and the surrounding area.

IF YOU'RE STAYING ONE DAY

Morning

Stop at City Hall.

Book your tour at the Laura Ingalls Wilder Memorial Society (if you have to wait, browse the gift shop or head across the street to the Discover Laura Center).

Meander up and down Calumet Avenue, taking the self-guided tour and imagining 1880s De Smet.

Stop in to the Loftus Store to examine their suspender collection (and other gifts).

Afternoon and evening

Shoot north of town to see Rose Wilder Lane's birthplace.

Swing back south to Ingalls Homestead. Make sure to get a glimpse of Silver Lake (off to the left) on the way.

Before the entrance to the Ingalls Homestead parking lot, pull over to wander among Pa's cottonwoods and up the hill to the memorial marker.

Marvel at the actual Big Slough across the road.

Get back in the car to drive the last little bit to Ingalls Homestead, enjoying the prairie until it's time to eat (time will vary depending on whether you're attending a pageant).

If you're going back to town for dinner, go a bit further to stop by the De Smet Cemetery south of town to see the Ingalls family's graves.

After dinner, either go back to the pageant site (near the cottonwoods) for your nighttime entertainment or take in a beautiful Dakota sunset at Ingalls Homestead.

IF YOU'RE STAYING TWO DAYS

Day 1

Morning

Stop at City Hall.

Book your tour for late morning at the Laura Ingalls Wilder Memorial Society.

Explore the exhibit behind the gift shop.

Hang out in the Discover Laura Center across the street.

Go on your tour, and at the end, take your time looking through the displays in the Third Street House kitchen.

Afternoon and evening

Meander up and down Calumet Avenue, reading the self-guided tour signs and imagining 1880s De Smet.

Visit the cemetery south of town and see how many names from the book series you can find.

Go back east on Highway 14. Find the Laura Ingalls Wilder Wilderness Trail at the intersection of Lyle Avenue and 4th Street and check out Silver Lake. Imagine geese flying overhead.

Continue on to Ingalls Homestead. Before the entrance to the parking lot, pull over to wander among Pa's cottonwoods and up the hill to the memorial marker.

Marvel at the actual Big Slough across the road.

Get back in the car to drive the last little bit to Ingalls Homestead, enjoying the prairie until it's time to eat or go to the pageant, or stay until the stars come out. (That's totally okay.) Don't forget to catch the Dakota sunset.

If you have time, invest 25 minutes in the drive to Arlington for a delicious dinner at the 1481 Grille.

Day 2

Morning

Grab breakfast to go in town and spend the early morning hours on Ingalls Homestead, imagining you're Laura in the 1880s.

Head north out of town and find Rose Wilder Lane's birthplace.

Keep going further north and find Spirit Lake.

Back in town, explore the Hazel L. Meyer Memorial Library and its extensive Laura Ingalls Wilder collection of literary artifacts.

Afternoon and evening

Stop by the Depot Museum and Harvey Dunn School and enjoy the prairie-inspired art.

Browse the Loftus Store for gift shopping.

Drive past Ingalls Homestead to turn further south to Lake Thompson. Pretend to be in a buggy.

Go back to Ingalls Homestead and enjoy the prairie until it's time to eat or go to the pageant, or stay until the stars come out—and enjoy that prairie sunset.

IF YOU'RE STAYING LONGER

Staying longer? These places and projects are well worth lingering over if you've got extra time:

The exhibit behind the gift shop the Laura Ingalls Wilder Memorial Society (displays vary)

The kitchen in the Third Street House

Hazel L. Meyer Memorial Library

The Gift Shop at the Laura Ingalls Wilder Memorial Society

Ingalls Homestead ... everywhere

A side trip to the remains of Manchester, where Grace Ingalls Dow lived, but was destroyed completely by a tornado in 2003

Pick up a copy of Wilder scholar Nancy Cleaveland's Laura Ingalls Wilder and Education in Kingsbury County or Charles Ingalls and the US Public Land Laws and use the maps therein to try to find the locations of the various homesteads and schools mentioned in the books.

Drive the road between Lake Henry and Lake Thompson.

Chapter 9
PARENTS' BURNING QUESTIONS

Where's the coffee?

To-go coffee is available at Ward's and The De Smet Mercantile and Coffeehouse.

Where's the restroom?

- **Ingalls Homestead** has restrooms on the grounds—in the gift shop, and in the storm shelter.
- Back in town, there are public restrooms right next to the People's State Bank on Calumet Avenue.
- On the east side of town there are restrooms available in the parking lot adjacent to the **4-H Park** across the street from the Laura Ingalls Wilder Memorial Society on Olivet Avenue, where the Historic Homes tours begin.
- Over on the west side of town, **Washington Park** (which also has camping) has bathrooms. Make sure you trek over there anyway to see the statue of Fr. Pierre Jean De Smet, the town's namesake.
- The gift shop of the Laura Ingalls Wilder Memorial Society
- The **De Smet Event and Wellness Center**, across the street from Washington Park, has restrooms as well.

Restrooms also exist in restaurants, but be a lamb and use them only when you are a paying customer of the establishment.

Where's the grocery store?

Maynard's Food Center is on Calumet Avenue at the north end of downtown, a few doors up from Ward's, on the left if you're headed north. It's smaller than traditional grocery stores, but is serviceable with most of the necessities you'd expect to find. But again, be warned—check what time it closes, as it might be earlier than you're used to.

Where's the pool?

De Smet has two pools—one at the Super Deluxe hotel (for hotel guests) and one public one for visitors, the De Smet City Pool. The City Pool is located on the south side of town, with open swimming is available in the afternoon and evening for a minimal fee, with a break in late afternoon for swim lessons.

Where's the ice cream?

De Smet Mercantile and Coffeehouse, the Oxbow, plus any of the convenience stores.

Where are the playgrounds?

There are three playgrounds in town.

The **4-H Park** is strategically located right across the street from the Laura Ingalls Wilder Memorial Society (which houses the gift shop) and Surveyor's House and adjacent to the Discover Laura Center.

On the west side of town, **Washington Park** is a large, lovely expanse of greenery that's well shaded. To find the playground equipment, look for the red structures. This park also has camping and restrooms.

On the northwest side of town, you won't find a blizzard cloud, but you will find **Rose Vincent Memorial Park**, the smallest playground in town. It has limited equipment, but if your kids are like mine, all they'll notice is "Hey! A playground!" It also has a basketball court and areas for picnicking.

You'll find a fun merry-go-round (the kind you push) at Ingalls Homestead.

Where are the ATMs?

Two ATMs in town are essentially across the street from one another, one at The Main Stop gas station, only accessible when the gas station is open, and one at the Dakotaland Federal Credit Union, available 24/7 next to the drive-up window. There's also one in Wheaties Bar and Grill.

Chapter 10
TRAVELERS'
COMMON CONCERNS

Oh no! I need linens!

If you've booked the covered wagon on Ingalls Homestead but forgot your linens, Walmart is in Huron, about 35 miles to the west. (Thus you should probably make every effort not to forget your linens.)

The grocery store isn't open!

De Smet is a small town, and unfortunately this means that the grocery store closes earlier than you might be used to. If you're planning on stocking your own food (particularly if you're trying to keep your kids eating semi-healthy), plan wisely and work in a pre-evening trip to the grocery store.

Restaurants aren't open on Sunday!

That's true, for some of them. Attractions are still open, though, and pageants happen on Sundays in July. If your travel includes a Sunday, plan accordingly and call in advance to find out what will be open.

So many mosquitoes!

As it happens, Mary could easily have eaten a bug in Dakota Territory if it was a mosquito. This part of South Dakota's everpresent sloughs are characterized in part by their standing water, so mosquitoes are unavoidable, especially at night. Since it's after dark, outdoors, and next to the Big Slough, De Smet's pageant is a veritable mosquito festival. Come prepared with repellent. (If you forget, pageant staff has been known to hand out repellent, but I wouldn't depend on it as a rule.) And dress for protection.

My kids don't like Laura Ingalls Wilder, but I do! Will they be bored?

It depends on the age. For tweens and below, even if your kids are not Laura fans, they will not be bored in De Smet. There are playgrounds for playing (bring a basketball and volleyball) and pools for swimming, and the Discover Laura Center is a must-visit for children from toddlers to school-aged. If you're staying at the Super Deluxe, they have a pool, and customers of Prairie House Manor can make great use of the front porch, which includes lots of toys for smaller children.

Then there's Ingalls Homestead. All ages, male and female—save for the most sullen of teenagers—will be able to have a good time at the Homestead. (My daughter is not a big fan of the book series, but she can't get enough of the kittens. Or the other animals, for that matter. She's also been known to bring a book and settle in the two-story barn to read.)

There is also a movie theater in Bryant, South Dakota, about 20 miles northeast via 25.

My other half doesn't like Laura Ingalls Wilder, but I do! What non-Laura activities are there?

Although Laura does have her male fans—William Anderson being the most prominent—it's true, the world of Laura Ingalls Wilder is primarily a girls' endeavor. Of course, not every little girl is a big fan, either. But there are a few ways the non-fans in your group might enjoy visiting De Smet anyway.

Fishing. Lake Thompson is great for fishing, especially walleye. It's just a short drive from De Smet and lodging is available there. Unfortunately, at this time boats are not available for rent. See the lodging section for further information on this spot.

Golfing. Non-residents of Kingsbury County can golf at the Kingsbury County Country Club and Golf Club for a fee. The golf club is a 5-minute drive (if that) south of town.

Hunting. Fall is hunting season, specifically for pheasants.

Wilder Field Airport. If anyone is a pilot or appreciates airplanes, several crop duster aircraft are hangared at the De Smet Airport on the same land that Almanzo Wilder had his tree claim. There is no FBO and the grounds are now gated and locked by FAA standards, but it's a joy for the spouse who needs to check out every little airport when on a trip.

Ingalls Homestead. For real. You do not have to be a fan of Laura Ingalls Wilder's books to be able to enjoy learning about or experiencing American pioneer history—or even just relaxing in the peaceful, expansive space.

De Smet Events Center. If your significant other needs to get some work done on the road, he or she can bring their laptop and use a workspace at the Center.

Can I really see everything?

Yes. De Smet is a tiny town, and you truly can accomplish this. To not give anything short shrift, do stay overnight. Stay for two nights, even three. Watch the prairie sunset, or catch a sunrise if you can. Go to church. Hit the town swimming pool. Make multiple visits to Ingalls Homestead. Take some time to feel the wind on your face, to contemplate rolling down the hill like a colt, Laura-style. Stand in the living room of the house that Pa built and marvel at the portrait of Caroline and Charles that hangs there. Shop in the Loftus Store and remember Pa's suspenders. Drive north and take in the homestead where Rose Wilder Lane was born. Stand on the rise of the prairie near where the Ingalls shanty stood on Ingalls Homestead and imagine you see Almanzo's buggy coming around the corner of Pearson's Livery Barn. It's all there for you to see, feel, and live, just as Laura did.

It's only fair that I warn you, though, and I apologize in advance.

Once you go, you'll always want to go back.

Acknowledgments

AS A LIFELONG FAN of Laura Ingalls Wilder's books I joked that I would travel the Little House® sites for my honeymoon (with no husband in sight). Leaving New England to marry, ironically enough, a western farmer meant something glorious: proximity to the Land of Laura. Or most of it, anyway. You can't know the feeling of your first walk across Ingalls Homestead, or seeing the sign for the Verdigris River in Kansas, or glimpsing the parlor wallpaper Eliza Jane patched for her brother in upstate New York until you're there, actually doing it. Fans know.

Thanks to my fellow Land of Laura travelers and beta readers Rachel, Sanne, Eddie, Melanie, Rebecca, Sue, Sarah, and Kim; the board of the Laura Ingalls Wilder Legacy and Research Association; my LauraPalooza peeps (I'd trade name cards with all of you anytime); Ann, Joan, Tim, and the entire Sullivan family; Bill Anderson and his perpetual support; and that gosh-dang farmer for actually using the word "Chinook" in regular conversation…and for not only enabling, but indulging.

About the Author

SANDRA HUME FIRST READ the Little House® series when she was nine. Twenty years later, she visited her first Laura Ingalls Wilder homesite. For a decade she published a twice-yearly print newsletter about Laura Ingalls Wilder, *The Homesteader*. In 2009, in the breakfast room of Prairie House Manor in De Smet, she became one of five founding board members of the Laura Ingalls Wilder Legacy and Research Association, which holds the academic- and fan-based conference LauraPalooza. She left the board in 2015 after six years of service. A professional writer and novelist, she lives in Colorado with her husband and three children.

APPENDIX
Resources

Many of these places have social media pages in addition to their official website. If a Facebook page, for example, is the only online presence an establishment has, I've included it. Otherwise, you can easily search for them.

TRAVEL AND CITY INFORMATION

City of De Smet and City Hall (geared to residents)
https://cityofdesmet.com
106 Calumet Ave
605.854.3731

De Smet, South Dakota (geared to tourists)
http://www.desmetsd.com
Community Guide to De Smet (available as a download):
https://desmetsd.com/pdf/2024_De_Smet_Community_Guide_Web.pdf
https://www.facebook.com/desmetsd

Travel South Dakota (request a free vacation guide)
800.732.5682
https://www.travelsouthdakota.com

Kingsbury Journal
220 Calumet Ave. SE
605.854.3331
https://www.kingsburyjournal.com
Map from the Laura Ingalls Wilder Memorial Society
https://discoverlaura.org/de-smet-map

PLACES OF INTEREST/ORGANIZATIONS

Wilder Welcome Center (not open regularly)
201 Calumet Ave SW

De Smet Pageant
http://www.desmetpageant.org

Laura Ingalls Wilder Memorial Society
105 Olivet Avenue
800.880.3383, 605.854.3383
http://www.discoverlaura.org

Ingalls Homestead
20812 Homestead Road
800.776.3594, 605.854.3984
http://www.ingallshomestead.com

The Loftus Store
205 Calumet Avenue
605.854.3773
http://www.loftusstore.com

Harvey Dunn Society
Facebook page:
https://www.facebook.com/harveydunnsociety/

De Smet City Pool
513 Loftus Ave. SW
605.854.9122

De Smet Depot Museum
104 Calumet Avenue
605.854.3991

Hazel L. Meyer Memorial Library
114 First Street SW
605.854.3842

First Congregational Church (Pa helped to build; now De Smet Christian and Missionary Alliance Church)
303 2nd Street

LODGING

Super Deluxe Inn
288 US-14
605.854.9388 or 877.687.7523
http://www.desmetsuperdeluxeinn.com

Prairie House Manor
209 Hwy 25 South
605.854.9131 or 800.297.2416
http://www.prairiehousemanor.com

Heritage House Bed and Breakfast
126 Calumet Avenue
605.854.9370
https://heritagehousesd.com

Cottage Inn Motel
Highway 14 & Calumet Avenue
800.848.0215

Lake Thompson State Park
21176 Flood Club Rd, Lake Preston, SD
800.710.2267
https://gfp.sd.gov (then navigate to the park's website)

North Shore Lodging and Campground (on Lake Thompson)
2603 North Shore Drive, Lake Preston, SD
605.690.5729
http://lakethompsonvacations.com

RESTAURANTS AND FOOD (DE SMET)

Check Facebook or Instagram for individual pages

Maynard's Food Center
107 Calumet Ave SE
605.854.3432

Restaurant at Kingsbury County Country Club
611 7th St SW
605.854.3134

Ward's Store & Bakery
217 Calumet Avenue NW
605.854.3688

The Oxbow
102 US 14 (Intersection of Highway 14 and Calumet Avenue)
605.854.9988
https://www.facebook.com/Oxbow1976/

Restaurant on Third Street (currently Half-Pint Steak and Spirits)
104 3rd St SW

The Dugout
123 Calumet Ave SE, De Smet, SD 57231
605.854.9171

Main Stop
102 US-14
605.854.9200

Cowboy Country Store
104 US-14
605.854.3553

OTHER DE SMET EVENTS

Harvey Dunn Plein Air Paint-Out
https://www.dunnpleinair.com

RESTAURANTS AND FOOD OUTSIDE OF DE SMET

Lake Preston Cafe
306 Main Ave. S, Lake Preston, SD
605.847.4605

1481 Grille
408 US-81, Arlington, SD
605.983.4630
http://www.1481grille.com

Cabaret
130 Main Street East, Carthage, SD 57323
605.772.9792

PLACES OF INTEREST OUTSIDE OF DE SMET

Corn Palace in Mitchell
612 North Main Street, Mitchell, SD 57301

866.273.2676 or 605.996.6223
http://cornpalace.com

Children's Museum of South Dakota in Brookings
521 4th Street, Brookings, SD 57006
605.692.6700
http://www.prairieplay.org/

South Dakota Agricultural Heritage Museum in Brookings
925 11th Street, Brookings, SD 57007
605.688.6226 or 1.877.227.0015
http://www.agmuseum.com

South Dakota Art Museum at South Dakota State University in Brookings (featuring a Harvey Dunn collection)
1036 Medary Ave., Brookings, SD 57007
605.688.5423
http://www.sdstate.edu/southdakotaartmuseum/

www.ingramcontent.com/pod-product-compliance
Lightning Source LLC
LaVergne TN
LVHW011338080426
835513LV00006B/416